Dear Hero,

Dear Hero,

poems **Jason McCall**

MARSH HAWK PRESS

East Rockaway, NY • 2013

13 14 15 16 17   7 6 5 4 3 2 1   FIRST EDITION

Marsh Hawk Press books are published by Poetry Mailing List, Inc., a not-for-
profit corporation under section 501 (c) 3 United States Internal Revenue Code.

Author photo by David A. Smith,
Book design and digital cover sketch by Claudia Carlson
(based on concept by Alice X. Zhang).
Text is set in Bembo and display in Frutiger.

LIBRARY OF CONGRESS CATALOGING-IN-PUBLICATION DATA

McCall, Jason.
Dear hero / Jason McCall. — 1st ed.
   p. cm.
Poems.
ISBN-13: 978-0-9846353-9-9 (pbk.)
ISBN-10: 0-9846353-9-4 (pbk.)
I. Title.
PS3613.C3449D43 2013
811'.6--dc23
                                        2012034096

Marsh Hawk Press
P.O. Box 206, East Rockaway, N.Y. 11518-0206
www.marshhawkpress.org

for Mom and Dad

Contents

Acknowledgements

Thankful acknowledgement is given to the following journals in which the poems listed below first appeared:

Abyss & Apex: "Nova" and "Wormhole"

Country Dog Review: "Job Description for Potential Hero Applicants"

Diverse Voices Quarterly: "Bizarro World" and "Con"

Fickle Muses: "Homecoming"

Flywheel Magazine: "Dear Hero, Along with the World, Please Keep the Following Items on Your Shoulders at All Times:"

Los Angeles Review: "Because Black Kids Can Read" and "Hero's Template for Dealing with Unruly Villains"

Peripheral Surveys: "Earth 2," "Earth Prime," "Underworld," "Watching *The Walking Dead* on the Anniversary of My Suicide Attempt," and "Zombieverse"

Specter Magazine: "Sidekick Funeral: John the Baptist" and "Sidekick Funeral: Ricky Baker"

Dear Hero,

Nova

Somewhere,
a star is dying.

And you are

here complaining
about the volume
of the band and dim
lights in the bar.

Prayer to Hercules as My Father Goes to War

Legend says we are the same
shoe size. Twin thirteens, unlucky

pair: is this bond strong
enough, son of Zeus?

Can you hear me when I kneel and plead
for my father? Dip his bullets

in the hydra's blood, place your lion
pelt over his shoulder and let the enemy's

missiles fall like feathers against his chest.
Make his voice rumble like your father's

storm clouds. Bend fate
to his favor as you bent the rivers

to clean the Augean stables. Lift him
to victory as you lifted the sky.

Sidekick Funeral: John the Baptist

Every MC needs a hype man,
Chuck D had Flav.
Biggie had Diddy.
And Jesus had you
to get the crowds ready,
to make sure the world knew
new shit was on the way.
You never loved yourself
too much or fell in love
with the idea that you could go
solo. You knew it wasn't about you;
it wasn't even about Jesus

and the whole "son of God"
tagline. It was about the message,
about the music of a million knees
dropping to the earth and dropping
their burdens at your boy's feet.
And that's why the message had to live
even if the body was on the cross,
in a Galilee grave, on his father's throne.
And you made sure the message pumped
through every speaker in heaven, hell, and earth.

Hero Wanted

Because we don't want our children
to dream of being us,
because we need you
to take the final shot,
to take the bullet
meant for our body,
to keep tonight still
and tomorrow pure,
to watch out for the drunk girls
at the end of the bar,
to make our weakness
look like divine will,
to make us hope
heaven can tell one speck of us
from another,
to help us believe
heaven cares enough
to save us from ourselves.

Job Description for Potential Hero Applicants

It's temp work, really, no benefits
or schedules. At any time, we may discontinue

our offerings to the gods or build a computer
that will surely go rogue and threaten humanity.

You will not be consulted on these decisions,
but we expect you to respond to them immediately.

It can be hard, but you're an orphan—
more likely than not—so roughing

it shouldn't be anything new.
If the forest is safe and that weird

cloud does not turn out to be an alien
assault armada, don't expect to hear from us.

We'll keep your name on file, though, scribble
it on neighborhood walls in case

anyone needs a hydra removed on short notice.
And if a job comes along and you manage

to save our town with your army
of gadgets you haul from quest

to quest because only full-time
members of society have storage privileges,

we will give you a pat on the back
with the same hand we reserve for garbage

men and janitors. We don't value you enough
to offer you a stable position, but don't give up.

Keep that sword strapped to your back;
keep waiting for us to remember your name.

Hector Rebukes the SEC Pregame Show

Defense wins championships.
Tell that to my father's corpse.
Tell that to my wife's new master.
Have you seen my home?

Have you seen my son
and the pieces of him
scattered amongst the broken walls
of my city? Try to defend

your home against god's hand.
Try to hold back the storm
with nails and sandbags
and prayers. Reinforce your citadels;

double your sentries. Beg heaven
to remember you and the omens
you discovered in the wind;
remember the gifts you left by the altar.

Wait for the gods to laugh
and order you to remember
there is only one omen:
that a man should fight for his country.

When the earth moves
against us, we can only charge
forward and hope
to leave a brave name.

Should You Accept Our Offer To Be a Hero

You will be allowed to fuck the prettiest girl
in town—once—and leave
her in the doorway dripping
tears in your footsteps.
She will find a man who won't make her
scream or hide the bruises
on her hip, and she will dream of you.

You will be known only
as the cloud who swallowed
the cloud blocking our sun.

You will not be given a date
for Homecoming, but you will
park your hot rod
on the hill above the gym
so that you can see the killer
coming in through the back door
and stop him just before he leaves
the queen in a puddle of lace and gore
and rhinestone.

You will enjoy holiday dinners
alone and stare at the phone only
twice; you will be strong.

Odysseus Gives His Debriefing

I trusted heaven, believed
the stars could see me
home—the same stars promised us Troy
would burn if we opened another virgin's
throat, gave our best
heifers to the sea. I knew the smoke
and cries would make it to Olympus
and make the gods notice
our blood. And they named me the wisest
of men while I stood with them throwing
wooden spears against stone walls
for a decade because the birds pointed east
or the boy king needed his glory
or because a cuckold couldn't keep his wife
in bed. I don't blame Zeus and his house; would you

listen to fathers wailing over broken sons?
Would any mother's curse matter
when Aphrodite is in your lap? How many ants
have you ground with your heel, melted
with a stare? That's the secret Delphi
won't give up. When the best of us pray—
the ones the world trusts
to grab the ear of heaven—
the gods don't answer us, either.

What a Dying Race Leaves Behind

"My teammates were like 'man, you're superman for real.' So that's
where the Superman name came from ... so everybody can know that
it wasn't me being like Shaq, it was 'cause I was lifting some weights."

—DWIGHT HOWARD

"Superman, my ass: make it a 'him versus me' thing. You tell me who the
real Superman is. If you want to bang and push, let's bang and push.
You're all giving away Superman titles; it's crazy."

—SHAQUILLE O'NEAL

"There ain't no such thing as a Superman."

—GIL SCOTT-HERON

Why do black kids bother to dream
so big? You'd think they could learn
to settle for a Batman or Iron Man.
They have movies; they save the world, too.
But what is a human body worth compared to Magic
Johnson's revelation, Ali's decay?
No, human bone and blood won't do;
they look to the sky for salvation,
for the savior their ancestors were promised
by the books and spirituals. They seek the rejection
of the earthly laws that say a man can't shoot
laser beams out of his eyes
or hold up a liquor store
overhead and use it to crush an army
of Bloodline Parasites or Manhunters.
What could they do if they were given a hand
strong enough to unravel a star,
skin stronger than steel?

Hero's Template for Dealing with Unruly Villains

Despite our best efforts to care
for all members of this world (good,
evil, and otherwise), you will find
that there will always be monsters
who do not follow the conventions
passed down to us by our fathers and fairytales.
You will encounter a werewolf howling on and on
about how he's special and how he's evolved
beyond the rules binding him to fire and full
moons. He will make a show, and society will look
to you for a response. Don't flinch; nervous heroes
create nervous hero worshippers. Be calm; find the right
time to pull the lycanthropic misanthrope aside
by his tail and remind him of the value of silver
bullets, sunlight, holy water, tradition.
Inform him that his disturbance is ruining the customs
of the people who pay good money to be here. Ask him what gives
him the right to make his own rules. Shame him,
and when he puts his head down and begins to turn
back into a bare, humbled man, raise your gun again.

Sidekick's Creed

If Superman is taken, I'll settle for a regular Dick
Grayson-Jimmy Olsen-John the Baptist role.

Someone has to stand next to the savior,
illustrate the difference between human and

super-human. Someone has to be the guy
who knew the Guy, saw the miracles, lived the legends.

What's a savior without the saved? Even our sins—
our little human fears and curiosities—glorify their names.

And there's a comfort in the shadow, a calm that comes
with the knowledge that nobody ever wants you

to stop the Joker's latest spree or turn water into
ice to stop Black Manta's invasion of Atlantis.

And there's the hubris, no doubt. Who dares
to befriend God, to learn nothing

from Icarus and Semele and Gwen Stacy,
to forget how fast flesh burns, how hard flesh falls?

Form Letter for Rejected Heroes

Thank you for being interested in saving us
from the bellies of wolves and the witches' boiling pots,
but after reviewing your application and ancestry,
we must inform you that your radiation-powered wet dreams

will never come true. No lightning exists
to feed you with the power of a million dwarves
going nova. You will never balance
a planet on your back. The universe does not tremble

at the thought of you awakening your dormant powers.
Your coming was not foretold in prophecy; no god
snuck his way into your mother's lap.
Your father is an electrician, and we do not believe this

will give you electrical abilities in the future. We wish
you the best of luck in finding a place for your talents,
and we encourage you to keep looking for magic
words in withered dictionaries, for swords forgotten in stone.

Sidekick Funeral: Patroclus

I learned fate loves some
more than others when my parents bought my brother
Reebok Pumps. He was meant to fly
off to college and carry the family name.

My feet were too small, his shoes too
big when I snuck them on and jumped
to palm the ceiling. We've all wanted to wear
our brother's shoes, our sister's hair. How heavy

was the crown of Achilles' helmet? You were sure it was
a sham when the Greeks cheered you on, followed
your chariot like you were the hero.
The Trojans even played along, dying

at the edge of your sword when you thought they would
die laughing at a serving boy aping
a hero's moves like some fool at the campfire
or king's court. You bought into the joke; you even

forgot it was a joke. You forgot the gods
made you to be fought over and carried by better men.
You forget you were another Helen,
another piece of youth cindered.

You didn't remember you were a man
until the god of light slapped you out of the dream
and Hector closed your eyes for good.
We see your form in the fire and promise vengeance

for every body given to the altar of war.
But we should see you and learn
better than to boast about being anything
other than kindling for the pyres.

I Hate Batman

Because he knows more karate moves
than I ever will, because my girl wants him
to fuck her in the Batmobile, because he can
stop Judgment Day with a flash
drive and fifteen minutes to plan.

But it's mostly because of the mask.
It could be Dunbar, but more
than likely it's the Malabar Road
summers rattling in my chest
when I see his logo; it's the clatter

of basketball games breaking down
into Trojan War standoffs when a swipe
at the ball turned into an eye poke.
We shouted our names; we claimed our neighborhoods;
we took off our masks and dared
our enemies to do the same.
There were no shadows to hide under; there was
nothing between us and the world
but the sweat that coated our frames
like armor and hung on our shoulders like capes.
When the adults pulled us apart, they would see
the madness in our faces and laugh,
but they would see our faces.

Con

At the sales rack, I swear I'm not
one of those guys who keeps a Superman shirt tucked
under his suit at interviews, who knows
the Green Lantern oath better than the Preamble.
My girlfriend claims me in the brightest days
and the darkest nights. I don't spend my weekends stroking
the glossy cover of the new *Power Girl* with one hand
and using the other to pump
the message boards with hate for any costume
that gained a new seam in the last decade. I wouldn't know
what to do with a pair of D&D
six-sided dice. I'm just passing
time until I find a real book,
until I figure out if Spider-Man and Mary Jane
can make it work, until Iron Man debuts
his new armor, until Wolverine gains his memory and loses
it again, until Superman finally proves he could destroy
Batman with a sigh, until I find something here
that doesn't remind me of something
I'm missing—a power I can't grasp, a secret
word too sharp for my tongue.

Work Order for Heroes

We know the moral behind teaching a man to fish
instead of giving him the fish, but we're hungry.
And there's a man-eating
octopus in the town lake. Yes, it is

true, we should have been taking notes
the last time you wrestled the boogeyman
back under our beds, but we were praying
with our eyes closed or texting with our eyes

open so our friends could know about the OMGWTF!
moment when you suplexed a minotaur
through a table. But we never learned
our lessons, never learned the magic word

that keeps reanimating the mummies,
never learned which pool has a kraken at the deep end.
So we need you one more time. We promise
it's just one more time.

Because Black Kids Can Read

comics too, I'm the conscious colored, dark
and wise, the suntanned wingman. Like Iron Man,
but with more guns and less
brains or the Green Lantern who willed
himself out of the ghetto. I'm bursting
through the wall when the hero needs me,
carrying the cliffhanger of War Machine

vs. Doctor Doom! Falcon
vs. Red Skull! Steel vs. Darkseid! No, I won't
save the day, only keep the action going,
keep the message boards warm while the man
on the cover recalibrates his armor or finds
out why his powers didn't work the last issue.
Either way, I'll be found in a pile of rubble
with a villain standing over me making jokes
about Jesse Owens. The real hero

will return to avenge me, and then it's back
to the mansion until it's my turn
for the special issue that shows me cleaning up
my neighborhood and saving my siblings
from the street gang led by my childhood
best friend. I'll show the brothers
drugs and thugs are as bad as a Lex Luthor lovechild
with Lady Deathstrike, and, if they stay in school
and follow the rules, they can be second-class
superheroes, just like me.

Sidekick Funeral: Aeris

The world doesn't work
like this. The sword wasn't real—a line

of pixels stabbing a block of polygons—
but the shock was real. My grandmother

died in March, but you were the first lesson
we learned about death that year. We could accept

chickens running on water
with messiahs on their backs. Shiva

and Odin on speed dial. But we couldn't believe you
would never come back. The world played Orpheus,

digging into the deep
corners and looking for answers.

Every rumor was an incantation,
a false oracle swearing you would come back

if we could find the right potion,
find the right god to summon you back.

Wormhole

The shortest space
between us is a cooperative heaven.
And I will dare

reaching into the universe
and its sly belly as long as you are
on the other side.

Parallel Universe

Do we ever really wake up
in the same world we left

behind for our dreams?
The new day gives us cancer

in our throat, a god
in our bellies, a plan to crash

a plane through an embassy wall.
Every time someone stops us

and says "I remember you,"
it's a lie. Cells die and resurrect;

brains wrinkle and decay past the point
of salvaging. Mary was not the mother

of god until she was. John Wilkes Booth only acted
until he acted. One day, Clark Kent winced

from the pop of his father's fastball
in his glove. The next day, Clark Kent snapped

a black hole in half with his thumb.
Captain America is a black, blonde, Russian spy.

"And then one day" is always today
for one of us. We will all find ourselves

spit into bodies too big for our hopes
and feet allergic to solid ground.

Earth 616

I can give up on Superman
and Black Adam; My name is good enough.
I command the dead with a whisper.
I speak to ghosts in every world,

but they listen here. I don't care how many worlds had to die
to get to this point, how many mistakes
of fate or providence placed this earth
in the Goldilocks Zone where the temperature is just right

and I have the power to make the Hulk lose sleep. I'm even
a preacher. Dad can remember this job; he doesn't
need reminders when cousins ask during the holidays.
By day, I preach the gospel. By night, I scroll the obituaries

like Sunday sales papers in search of a minion
who can cook a mean batch of macaroni
or fix an engine. You'd think I would never get tired
of making the ghost of Marilyn Monroe hula-hoop

or listening to Macho Man and Andre the Giant argue
over whose Wrestlemania III match meant more.
Why can't this be my home?
Because you're not here. I can't order you to rise

from the grave any more than I can erase your scent
from the couch or throw your razors out of the tub.
I am Jason McCall, the Soul Man. I am
Orpheus, Odysseus, and every stupid man

who plays the hero brushing
Death aside to catch a strand of your hair
before the universe remembers we weren't supposed to be
anything more than dust.

Earth S

I was at the bus stop wishing I was Captain Marvel when you showed up. It would have been perfect if the temperature was three degrees lower and you were sitting four inches closer to me. It would have been perfect if my breath didn't smell like last night's cheap gin and hesitation. I would have cleaned the grit out of my eyes if I had known I was going to see you here; I would have ironed my shirt. I wish I could have whispered a magic word and gained the wisdom of Solomon and known the right things to say, where to begin. Or Mercury's speed would have let me string together a sonnet before you stepped on the bus and the driver closed the door between us. But I needed more to unclench my jaw. I needed the strength of Hercules. Hell, I would've settled for Samson as long you agreed to be my Delilah. I don't have much hair, but I'd leave the scissors on the table for you. Darling, take your time.

Atlantis

There's a reason the world needs
water, the first connection
between mother and child.
How do you know if life is possible
beyond our soggy rock? We search
for signs on broken planets and see our parents,
our children, proof of our gods.
We were all born swimming, and we all
remember the flood, the wave
pushing us apart forever and claiming
the only home we ever knew.

Earth 811

With a zeal greater than John
Connor, my niece—sock-gloved
and ski-masked— pushes away my midnight
cereal and begs me to help her bust up some robots.
I refuse. She says she doesn't care
if they are Autobots or Decepticons, Ultron clones,
Braniac probes, Gundam suits, Visions from the future,
Manhunters, Red Tornado fragments, Skynet HKs,
Red Ribbon androids, Doombots, Hephaestian automatons,
Omega sentinels, sentient Iron Man armors,
or GPS systems that give too much lip
when we miss a turn. Finally, I have to
tell her it's too late to fight machines,
and we go sleep disappointed.

Zombieverse

This land is a prom-movie pastiche
where we learn to appreciate brains
and that beauty is skin deep. And the skin peels
at the thinnest touch, along with the rest
of what holds us together. That's the real horror:
a world of dead skin covering the coffee table,
unkempt lawns, boutique doors
cracked and smeared. Who's left

to keep up with all of the sick
days? Who will leave warnings
on the cars parked at meters long after
the two hour limit? How will the children survive
missing so many days of math?

Earth 2

We see the face of Batman
on the obituary page, and Superman is too

weak to keep the Just
for Men: a Touch of Gray out of his cart

as he shuffles through the Metropolis
Mega-Mart. Time exists. Hands move

over the creased photos of your first love
who got fat, got married, got killed

at the intersection where you first tasted
another person's tongue. And that place is sacred,

a crude cross and dead flowers acting
as an altar and offering both prayer and warning

for the world: your heroes will turn
to dust, and you will beg

to know how we ever managed
to become so small.

Underworld

This is where we face our skeletons,
dress our fears of the horizon
in bed sheets and goat horns. No, this is
where we let our heroes face the skeletons
of our fathers and beg them to give
details when they return from the other
side intact. We learn resurrection and the law
of conservation. All things buried will scrape

their path back into the world as a zombie
army, host of a demonic avatar, the ghost
wearing your lover's face each morning. The weak
earth pays no mind to wickedness or good
works; sinners and saints are not sorted in the bowels
of Avernus, Elysia, or whatever
place we dream of to give our dead
a fitting home. In this land, we let bodies turn
back to imagination before they reassemble, like the dew
becoming vapor becoming the cloud
carrying tomorrow's storm.

Earth AD

With Tuscaloosa guilt for being born
a tiger, I bathe in crimson
gore. All muscle and fire, lonely
as a Clint Eastwood protagonist,

my claws grow sharp on bark and bone.
My feet drop like snowflakes; my jaw
drops like god's bolt.
The other animals talk

and pay taxes and wear pants.
I stay on all fours like a fanatic
in praise of the god who put blood
in my nostrils and a bear under my paw.

Mangaverse

We show our true selves
only in crisis.

When your man leaves
you at the keg party, you call a giant
robot to cut the frat house in half
with a plasma blade.

When you hear *nigger*
on the wind as you walk to class, you summon
the fury of your forefathers, cradle the heat
of a million Alabama suns in your fists.

When you bury your last hope in this world, you sprout
a voice that roils the seas,
stills the stars.

When you must know the origin of your birthmarks
and scars, you crack the earth
searching for a root.

Bizarro World

Everything is backwards—
spheres become cubes,

Marilyn Monroe is the ugliest
woman in the world—so I am

an only child, female, probably
from some place like Oregon

that ranks high in literacy
and low in diabetes. Here, I took

my high school counselor's advice
and became an actuary who can count

the number of times she's put out
on the first date, who can turn her head

away from a *Rocky* marathon.
I talk about bootstraps and emerging markets;

I know the difference between scallions and scallops.
I don't buy Shaq albums; I can

beat Mario and Mega Man and finish
every poem I start with my eyes closed. But I don't

know that because I have no time
for games in this world,

no time for pretending I could be anything
other than what I am.

Earth 3

You are a Cassandra—your fears turned prophecy. You told the world that the world was falling to hell, and now you're one of the only ones left to feel the lick of the flames. And now, there's a black man at your door. You've heard of his kind, but you assumed the quarterbacks were all athletics and no acumen, the CEOs were an affirmative action show. But your locks are picked; he whistles as he types in your security code just before the siren rings to alert the neighbors, to call the empty police station. You want to call out for help, wish for a world where Superman exists to save you. But Superman does exist. And he's in your backyard. And he's laughing at the angle of your dog's head after snapping its neck. You are paying for paying your taxes, for keeping the skateboarders out of the parking lots and the syringes out of the sandboxes, for giving every kid a chance in the school spelling bee. Now, the intruder steps into the light of your bedroom, disassembles the gun shaking in your hands, and spells out his plans for you. "Open. O-P-E-N. Open. Your. Y-O-U-R. Your. Mouth. M-O-U-T-H. Mouth." He tells you, one letter at a time, how you made him become the Enunciator when you kept him out of the fourth grade spelling bee. He tells you he sought out to learn the root of all things. "Did you know that 'teach' and 'revenge' share the same origin? What about 'villain' and 'home'?" You know now. And now you know how your mouth works again. And now you hope to scream for help, scream for this world, scream because you imagine some part of your voice will reach another kindred and kind soul in time to save your body from the crows and ants. And now he pulls a black hole out of his pocket and sets it on your tongue.

Earth Prime

You hear the neighbor girl screaming again and hope
she's having sex. Ignore the bumps
and shattered glass. It sounded like glass,
but you're not sure because this is the real world.

You're no hero; you're too busy
to call the cops and too weak to break the lock.
And what would that do for your security
deposit? There is no god

planting a savior in a virgin's belly;
there is no alien messiah
or magic ring that's going to find
your hand and make you forget

about the wife you should have.
There is only the angel
catching your fist when you go to knock
on the door, the same guardian that keeps you

out of the park after sundown,
keeps you away from tequila and high school
classmates because your origin story shouldn't be
retold, because the only power god wanted

to give you was the power of denial. And you use
that gift to make the world make-believe, to make
sure those screams are only passion
pushing through your duplex wall.

Homeworld

I told my girlfriend about waking up inside other women and men, and she decided to leave an address on the nightstand and a kiss on my cheek. The address was a doctor's office in the back room of a Super Target. And the doctor was Scott Bakula. Of course, he knew all about changing bodies, possessing and being possessed. I nodded and replied in turn; I could do the doctor-patient dance. There were no rookies in this room. But I didn't know if Bakula understood due to his time on *Quantum Leap* or because body snatching was part of being an actor. He said we're all looking for some version of home as he patted me on the back and pushed me through the door. The mention of home made me hear my brother laughing while we watched old shows and swept roaches from the pallet that was our bed, theater, magic carpet. And for the first time in a long time, I knew I was in my own body; my thoughts were my thoughts, and I had no one else to blame for the stray pieces of spirit rattling in my stomach like dropped wrenches and screws.

Horizons

If the universe is still
expanding in the face of dying
stars, why did you stop reaching?

Heroic Guidelines for Dating on the Job

The world is your work
space, so all relationships will be a conflict
of interest. Your sons will hack at your shadows

until your legacy is left ribbony and raw;
your daughters will burn
cities with a flash of an ankle.

But even with this knowledge,
we expect you will let a lover or two slip
their names into your chest

deeper than any blade can reach.
The wounds will fester, leave you bedridden
and bloated. Your sword will grow

dim and dull, your ears slack
to the wails of the needy.
"Who needs you more than us?" the family

will ask, and you will not manage
an answer, and you will pretend
the screams of the dying are stray winds

rattling your door. And the lie will grow
until your whole world is a little house
where feats are measured by the balance

of dishes on a forearm, fevers cured
with a kiss. And your past will finally fall
into memory—the pits, skeletons, flecks of flesh—

until it returns as boot prints and blood
leading to a severed head and a note from a jilted
foe. This will be your greatest test

of strength. How many times can you lift the earth
and carve a grave? Can you stand to count the bodies
you leave under your feet?

Sidekick Funeral: Stonewall Jackson

You had to die for the dream
to live. A Southern man, you know the lord;
you read Abraham and Exodus. Sometimes,

God won't take any payment but blood.
If you lived past Chancellorsville,
what good would you be? Your soldiers

ground to nothing under Sherman's boot,
your last days spent under an Oklahoma sun
or a Mississippi hood. No,

we couldn't have that,
but we couldn't have your blood
on a Yankee bullet, either.

If the South could ever rise again,
we had to bury some of our own,
sow them into the earth and pray for light.

Hector Reenlists at the Local 7-Eleven

They said, "Give up
the money. A few dollars
ain't worth a life."

These are the orders
my parents give to me every night
before I go to greet violence.

Then why am I here
wearing this bronze shield
on my chest, this badge

announcing my name
and obligation?
They want me to hide

behind the wall
and wait for better men
to arrive, men blessed

with better armor, stronger arms.
But a defender gives nothing.
Giving up the beach damned us

more than Odysseus' mind
or Achilles' ashen spear.
I killed the first enemy

who landed on my shore.
I didn't wait to hear the cry of his family
tree and formal challenge.

He could have been a cook;
he could have been a distant cousin.
I only knew he wanted

what I swore to protect.
What more reason
does a soldier need?

When I Cleaned Tables at Applebee's

to pay for Spring Break and karate lessons,
a waiter told me I was too smart
to be a busboy, suggested I'd be better off serving
my country on a nuclear submarine
and using my Algebra III skills to calculate
missile strikes. I could
show the towelheads how America deals
with fear. I laughed it off, mumbled
something about writing between mouthfuls
of garlic bread and Coke. He asked why not write
about killing terrorists with missile strikes.
Why not be another shrouded hero,

hide like the Greeks at Troy and pray to the sea
god for protection? Or why not be Apollo
and hurl death from an unseen heaven?
This power was mine as long as I was brave
enough to solve polynomials and take a swim class.
I never had the heart
to be a ghost or god or guard my homeland
from a world away. I knew I could never kill
a man before I knew his face.

My Fear Can Beat Up Your Fear

We manufacture mindless
predators to hunt
down faceless terror.

We signal for Batman
to clear the shadows
from the night alleys.

We keep Mechagodzilla
tuned up just in case
the original goes rogue. Again.

We pray Hercules will find time
to wrestle our monsters between his bouts
of infanticide and Amazon rapes.

We carve our mothers into
gods because only a god can heal
a four inch cut with a kiss.

How do we deal with dread?
We cast nightmares
to protect our dreams.

International Conference for Heroes and Heroic Studies

At home, you were special, but everyone here is
the son of some god, some authority
on Sphinxian rhetoric or the Early Childhood Development

of demigods. At the hotel bar, you all
trade tales of your mothers riding
bulls, being bent over by shadows, writhing

in mists. And you share stories of rejection, submitting
to the weight of blood, applying Orpheus' logic
to every playground split or garage band divorce.

The next day, your panel discussion on Trojan War epithets
in the age of Twitter is attended by three people;
one of them is a warlock in disguise who challenges

you with anecdotes from the netherworld
that can't be substantiated. But you can't call him out
and kill him because of the non-violence pledge

attached to your application. Heroes keep their word,
and that's why you are stuck
slow dancing with the elf you met in the air

line shuttle on the way to your hotel.
You promised her a dance because she was pretty;
you didn't realize all the girls here would be pretty.

Later, she will pin you down and force you
to think of the skulls stapled to your wall back home,
all of the times your name has been called in vain

while you have been away.
Before she leaves, you will pray for her
to bite you until you both taste blood.

Krakoom

Makes Thor mighty, turns Adam
black again, lets amoeba grow into man. Heat
required for change. Remember the old story

of us being stuck together in the beginning, lover
to lover, until the gods became fearful
or jealous or just tired of watching us and split

the world with thunderbolts. We didn't learn
that trick until 1945. Car shocks
my hand in winter, and there's Phaeton

driving his dad's chariot with the license
only dumb boys can carry. I suck my thumb
and decide it could be worse.

Dessert burned my mouth last night and I felt
you again, the piece of lightning curled
around my tongue. Let's share an apple

and pretend the fall never happened.
If we step lightly, we can walk into space
on a sunray and watch the world rewind.

Watching *The Walking Dead* on
the Anniversary of My Suicide Attempt

I don't know who to cheer for: the last shreds of humanity—running from broken home to broken home, boarding up windows and making last stands in alleyways—or the horde of flesh that refuses to die. Who has the right to see the morning? What makes us fear the undead? It's not the brain eating; it's the betrayal. The dead don't walk. What is buried should remain buried. We see the hordes and imagine our own secrets and treasures and loves unearthed and out of our control. What have I buried? A grandmother. Internet search histories. A photo album of me and a girl I should have married. She was only honest when she talked about death. My girlfriend grabs me when zombies break a window, when the hero's gun misfires. I don't flinch. I know these monsters are real; I know what they can do. The show's got it all wrong: they can run on treadmills; they can lecture on Romanticism and the rise of the graphic novel. They remember their lives. They know they're breaking the rules of this world with every piece of flesh they leave behind. She hides her face in my chest when the frenzy begins. Intestines are pulled out and keep going like magic scarves. Someone always loses their heart. She asks me how I can watch a show like this. I say it's because I'm a man, but that's a lie. I watch because it's a mirror; I watch because the mirror is too sharp. I watch to learn how to survive.

Sidekick Funeral: Ricky Baker

We were all running with you
in that alley, little
brother, every one of us

who chased a job that was gone the second
the secretary barked "can I help you?"
and demanded to see ID, every one of us

who couldn't pay for condoms and now
can't afford a car seat because we blew our wad
on Ruby Tuesday and haircuts for prom, every one of us

who had to pretend it was fun
sleeping on the floor
for three years, every one of us

who begged our friends not to read
the tags on our jeans or the tongue
of our shoes, every one of us

who thought we could outrun this world
until the sun marked us black
and cut through our dreams like a shotgun.

Plea of Hercules

I was born killing
animals, threatening
the unconquerable sun.
I killed my first teacher,
but you swore I would learn
to guide my strength.
You called it flashes of my father
and his temper, said I would calm
like the rest of his storms.
The signs were all there.
What did you expect me to do
when I felt lightning

racing in my blood?
Can you plan for a thunderbolt;
can I be anything more than a weapon
in this world that cracks like dry wood
under my feet? You are all kindling.
If my arms can crush stars,
imagine the scene of me cradling
a child, cupping a breast.
How can you blame fire?
You should have burned me
the second I told you about god
hiding under my skin.

Heroine

Somewhere, a marine is shooting
a burger wrapper into a trashcan or shooting
into homes in Mosul.
I was supposed to marry you. Drunk
in frat house basements—our faces smashed
together because we were the only black faces—
you always held my hand
before it went where it didn't belong,
told me to be patient, told me you were worth the wait.
You promised to take care of me one day,
said you'd do all the work while I sat back
and wrote poems like this one.
Once we finished school, we'd finish
what we started on so many weekends
but never finished because my friends pulled me away
or because you passed out before I could find a condom
or an open Taco Bell.
I stopped believing in muses when you left me
for the war; I stopped thinking about you until
I saw the last soldiers leave Iraq. Michelle,
you did take care of me, me and the rest of this world.
Thank you for your promises; thank you for keeping
my hands in place.

When I Forget My Driving Glasses

I can almost see myself
as Superman, tearing through

the city to save my girlfriend
who asks too many questions

from the threat of cramming
for exams on an empty stomach.

I don't feel like I could crush a star
or outrun a blade of sunlight, but I do

feel dangerous, like a drunk
with speed dial, a southpaw

boxer, a coach who kills kids
with one more suicide run

to build character, prom night
without protection, a baby

Oppenheimer.
The split

happens here. If
my eyes that can't scan

an optometrist's chart
fail, if my hands that can't bend

steel slip from the wheel,
my body will be another pile of dirt,

just like the plots he plowed in Smallville
before he found his strength.

The Heroes I Know Never Come Home

wearing another man's armor,
dragging captive wives and children
behind them in a victory chain. They don't talk
much about immortal fame or leaving
their enemies for the dogs and crows.

They talk about lifting the giants
their babies have become out of minefields
of cracker crumbs and juice.
The babies aren't giants; they're just so much bigger
than they were when the heroes left home
to make sure the giant babies had a world
to grow into.

They talk about boobs:
Rihanna's boobs, Katy Perry's boobs,
how they've become experts on Benjamin
because they know real boobs can't be copied
by a digital camera or T1 line.

They talk about the alchemy
it took to turn sand
into whiskey, Pop
Tarts into batteries.

They talk about the upcoming season,
which back looks good enough to carry us
all the way. They talk about wins and losses
and all things in a language we will never know.

Sidekick Funeral: Bucky Barnes

We didn't want you back.
Your blood mattered. "Only Bucky
stays dead." It was a mantra, a lesson
in consequence, a lesson of how Freedom
names the best of us as her price.
We chose you as our martyr, and you chose
to wake up in Moscow.
You could have been dead or you could have been Russian.
We were sure you'd pick the grave over the Reds.
You lived through the nightmare: the jackboots,
train stops, ashes, whispers of what
the world would be if Hitler got the bomb
or they got the U-boats to the shore.
But you woke up to something worse than a missing arm,

worse than lungs filled with arctic ice.
You learned to love
another nation's breast;
you hummed the enemy's anthem
before the big game, celebrated
the AK over the AR.
We can't decide if we want you
on the Avengers or on trial.
We're not sure when you'll run off
to settle some Cold War grudge.
We wanted to see you again, but
there's one good thing about dead bodies:
they stay where we leave them.

Furlough for Non-Deified Heroes

Nothing is guaranteed.
You know that more than most; I'm sure

that doesn't make this easier for you
or me. Every tomorrow makes

a liar out of today. I am trying
to say that we won't need you

this season. We never did
imagine the dragons

would stay in their lairs
and the toddlers would keep out

of the witches' kettles. But they did;
even the virgins are all claimed

and accounted for, and that never happens.
We hope you've kept your sword sharp

and kept up with the prayers
you've answered over the years.

They should come in handy now.
We heard the next town over might be on fire;

we gave your name to a shepherd who swears
his daughter was swallowed by the river.

We know the world needs you;
we just don't need you right now.

Termination Procedures for Excess Heroes

When the enemy surrenders to your will,
we will ask you to surrender your instincts.

When peace reigns over the horizon,
we will rein in your arms and armor.

When there's no need to lock our doors,
we will question why you have so many keys.

When you have slaughtered the last monster,
we will cringe at the gore under your nails.

When you return with horror in your mind and nightmare on your tongue,
we will muzzle you and beg you to keep these things out of our homes.

When you prove yourself greater than the mean hand of death,
you will find no place to live among us.

Homecoming

Only the dog recognized me when I came home.
Athena swears by the Styx it was because
of the disguise, but I know better
than to fall for one of her Goddess of Wisdom
mind-fucks. Even the gods forget who I am
sometimes. The wandering years I wear on my face
hide me better than any mask or shroud from Olympus.
When I wake up in the mornings and my body creaks
and groans louder than the old wooden bed,
I find it hard to believe that I was an equal to Ajax,
that my name once caused men to shudder in fear.
Penelope still says my name as a question:
Good Morning, Odysseus? I love you, Odysseus?
She is waiting for the day I reveal myself
to be just another unwanted suitor
who has invaded her home. In the evenings,
she still watches the sea, waiting for her husband
to return. I await his arrival more eagerly than she.

Thor Comes to Tuscaloosa

This is what happens when heaven touches earth.
When the sky fell from the sky, fate didn't
send a hero to set the odds. There was no Perseus
for this gorgon, no Superman for this Doomsday.
We were left to fight the bellow of judgment
with the whine of chainsaws, the hum of a fight song.
We made idols out of axe handles, hymns
out of every escape tale. We wanted
answers and help and something to watch
other than the impossible angles of the debris. And days

late, Thor showed his face, bonked the bad guys
on the head with his hammer, spun out
a whirlwind to clean up the mess,
and made me finally see my grandma
was right all along: God doesn't have blue eyes
and blond hair. God has an eye
that spins 200 MPH in every direction,
a mane of ruined oak and bone, and a face I can't stand
to see again.

The X-Men Come to Tuscaloosa

We know you're different—just
like the blacks and the queers and the cripples—

and when this is all over, the servers will go back
to spitting in your beer and the cops will swear

your turning light didn't blink just like they do
to the blacks and the gays and the cripples.

But for now, just now, we don't care
if you can talk to computers or run at Mach 5

or see through our bedroom walls or
raise the dead. Can you swing an axe without cutting

your leg in two? Can you move this mountain of ice
inside before it melts?

The Lantern Corps Comes to Tuscaloosa

When our blackest night came in the afternoon,
Fear was not a blob chewing

through skyscrapers and souls until Van Wilder
flew it into the sun. It was a mother

in a dark parking lot with a dead
phone and a daughter in a field across town.

She hoped. It was me praying for her daughter as I folded
laundry and debated if I should buy a baby

pampers or formula, if I should hold on
to the receipt, if the guardians of the universe exist

just to save me, an empty stadium, a Wendy's,
if Sinestro was able to track down the tornado

and give it the yellow ring it earned by spinning terror
across the state with every piece of limb

and rubble. It was me lying still
in the stillest night, flexing

my ear to catch the first hum of a generator,
the first creak of the new day.

The Transformers Come to Tuscaloosa

The last time I cried was on Christmas.
My brother got an Optimus Prime;
I got a Dinobot. What else
am I supposed to think about when humvees

and helicopters cover my old neighborhood?
When "How's the football team?"
is replaced by "How are you?"
"How's the town?" "How did you make it?"

I used to want a giant robot
that could turn into a handgun;
maybe that's why I failed
physics. But now, I don't want a gun,

or any fancy car with cosmic bass, or a pastel
colored fighter jet. I want the front
load shovels, bulldozers, dumpster trucks,
and excavators to merge into Devastator

and chomp through every stray cinder
block and split tree like they are grape
flavored energon cubes. I know it
can't happen. But this can't be happening, either.

Captain America Comes to Tuscaloosa

Here we go: one more Yankee
on steroids pretending he's better than us,

telling us what flag we should fly
in our yards, what men we can let live

next door. Thank you for punching Hitler
in the face, and thank you for stopping the Nazi

bomb headed for the East Coast, but we don't need you
giving us lectures about fighting for home,

about when it's time to give up our guns,
about being stuck in time. Every bomb

and dog bite and baseball bat dressed
in a black boy's brains gets frozen like wedding cake

and unthawed whenever some Poly-Sci major
from Oregon writes "nigger" on a bathroom stall

as part of her dissertation research. But you wouldn't
know about that, would you, Cap? I'm sure

the only colors you see are red, white, and blue.
I'm sure you just want to help us win this fight.

Conan Comes to Tuscaloosa

Even though you will name us cowards for not fighting
reason and science to claim vengeance over the storm,
I'm sure the ruins will make you feel
right at home. And the lamentations of the women

have not ceased. The men have been lamenting, too,
but they will wipe the tears away before they look you in the face
and swear they don't need help lifting the tree
out of their living rooms. See, we believe in independence like you.

We believe in becoming kings or rebels or bandits
by our own hands; we believe in shaping our own
fate. So don't be surprised by the rejections,
but don't expect them to stop you

from sorting the iron and stone like you were trained
to do by the war masters of the East.
And you should learn something
about football before you come to town.

Everyone will beg you to tryout for the team;
they'll tell you we need a pass rush and you would be perfect
at defensive end. There's no need to puff up
your chest and give a booming speech about how you never play

defense and how you always belong at the center
where the battle is thickest and not at the edges
like some horsemen or archer. Let us give you a compliment,
and please let us lean on your strength.

Dear Hero, Along with the World, Please Keep the Following Items on Your Shoulders at All Times:

The curse, the quest, the blessed
weapons, the father watching
from afar, the beasts, the sidekick
funerals, the certainty of continents
splitting under hand, the gore
that won't wash off the shoes, the promise
of heaven, the hidden powers,
the wives, the legion of unanswered pleas,
the shadow-eating sons, the statues,
the rumors growing fat as earthworms
waiting to eat a godly corpse and swear
it tasted just like a man.

Notes: A Guide to Parallel Universes

"Earth 616." On Earth 616, gamma radiation—the same radiation that transforms Bruce Banner into the Incredible Hulk—transforms Father Jason McCall into Soul Man. As Soul Man, Jason McCall has the power to resurrect the souls of the dead.

"Earth S." Earth S is protected by Billy Batson and the Marvel family. When he speaks the word "SHAZAM!" he transforms into Captain Marvel and is granted the wisdom of Solomon, the strength of Hercules, the endurance of Atlas, the power of Zeus, the courage of Achilles, and the speed of Mercury.

"Earth 811." Sentinels, the robotic enemies of the X-Men, rule Earth 811, and most of their opposition is dead or imprisoned.

"Earth 2." Batman is dead, and the other heroes are old. Later on, Superman dies, too.

"Earth AD." After the Great Disaster on this planet, humans are enslaved by intelligent, humanoid animals.

"Bizarro World." Bizarro World is the inverse of this world. And, at any given time, it is inhabited, created, or destroyed by Bizarro, an imperfect clone of Superman.

"Earth 3." Here, all of your heroes have become villains.

"Earth Prime." Earth Prime is this world, the world we all dream of escaping.

Photo by David A. Smith

About the Author

Jason McCall is from the great state of Alabama, where he currently teaches at the University of Alabama. He holds an MFA from the University of Miami, and his poetry has been featured in *Cimarron Review, Fickle Muses, The Los Angeles Review, New Letters, Poems & Plays*, and other journals. His previous collections include *Silver* (Main Street Rag) and *I Can Explain* (Finishing Line Press).

Titles From Marsh Hawk Press